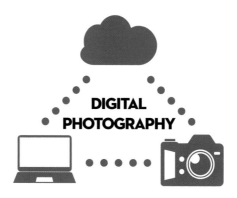

DIGITAL PHOTOGRAPHY

ASTROPHOTOGRAPHY

By John Hamilton

Abdo & Daughters
An imprint of Abdo Publishing | abdopublishing.com

abdopublishing.com

Published by Abdo Publishing, a division of ABDO, PO Box 398166, Minneapolis, Minnesota 55439. Copyright © 2019 by Abdo Consulting Group, Inc. International copyrights reserved in all countries. No part of this book may be reproduced in any form without written permission from the publisher. Abdo & Daughters™ is a trademark and logo of Abdo Publishing.

Printed in the United States of America, North Mankato, Minnesota.
082018
092018

THIS BOOK CONTAINS
RECYCLED MATERIALS

Editor: Sue Hamilton
Copy Editor: Bridget O'Brien
Graphic Design: Sue Hamilton
Cover Design: Candice Keimig and Pakou Moua
Cover Photos: iStock & John Hamilton
Interior Images: Canon USA-pg 12 (top); Deposit Photos-pgs 24 & 31; Dylan O'Donnell-pgs 39 (bottom) & 41 (bottom); EAGTAC-pg 36 (inset); Eastman Kodak-pg 6 (top); iOptron-pg 39 (top); iStock-pgs 4-5, 6-7, 8, 11 (top), 13 (bottom), 14, 15 (top), 16, 17 (bottom), 18, 20, 21, 23, 25, 28, 29, 32, 33, 34-35, 36-37, 40, 42, 43 (top) & 45; John Hamilton-pgs 15 (bottom), 19, 26-27, 38 & 41 (top); Nikon USA-pgs 9 (inset), 10, 12 (center), 13 (top), 14 (inset), 15 (inset), 16 (inset) & 17 (cord & battery); SanDisk-pg 17 (memory card); Science Source-pg 22; Shutterstock-pgs 9, 11 (bottom) & 30; Sony Corporation of America-pg 12 (bottom); U.S. Copyright Office-pg 43 (bottom).

Library of Congress Control Number: 2017963909
Publisher's Cataloging-in-Publication Data
Names: Hamilton, John, author.
Title: Astrophotography / by John Hamilton.
Description: Minneapolis, Minnesota : Abdo Publishing, 2019. | Series: Digital photography | Includes online resources and index.
Identifiers: ISBN 9781532115851 (lib.bdg.) | ISBN 9781532156786 (ebook)
Subjects: LCSH: Astronomical photography--Juvenile literature. | Space photography--Juvenile literature. | Photographs from space--Juvenile literature. | Photography--Digital techniques--Juvenile literature.
Classification: DDC 522.63--dc23

CONTENTS

CAPTURING THE NIGHT SKY

Photographers have aimed their cameras toward the heavens ever since film was invented. However, it has only been recently that astrophotography has really taken off. Digital cameras have revolutionized the way people capture the stars and planets. Now almost anyone with the right equipment and know-how can take breathtaking pictures of the Moon, meteor showers, or the magnificent Milky Way galaxy.

Today's digital cameras capture a level of detail, color, and range of light that didn't seem possible just a few years ago. A new generation of photographers has rekindled an interest in astronomy. This comes at a time when fewer people can see the stars, thanks to the growing light pollution of our cities. Astrophotography is a way to bring back the wonders of the night sky and remind us of its beauty.

BEGINNER'S GUIDELINES

Learning astrophotography can be hard. There are technical details to master, and a lot of gear to become familiar with. The most important thing is to get to an interesting location and just have fun. We learn through trial and error. Luckily, with digital cameras, there is no film to waste, and mistakes can be corrected on the spot.

6 TIPS FOR WHEN YOU ARE STARTING OUT

1. There's no need to buy fancy equipment right away. Use the gear you already own. The only "must have" is a good, sturdy tripod.

2. Know how to control your camera. You don't want to fumble around in the dark trying to work unfamiliar buttons and knobs.

3. Start out shooting the full Moon and nightscapes with bright stars at twilight. These are relatively easy shots for beginners. Move on to more advanced astrophotography as you learn through experience.

4. Learn how to process RAW images (not JPEGs) in editing software such as Lightroom or Photoshop. It is not too difficult, and will make a world of difference in your final images.

5. Read a book about astronomy and get familiar with the night sky. Which constellations are visible during which seasons? Free software such as Stellarium can help you figure out what stars are visible in the night sky wherever you live, during any season.

6. You'll have to travel outside the light pollution of major cities. Get out to the country, or a wilderness park, far from city lights.

CAMERAS

Digital photography captures a scene when light passes through a lens and is focused onto an image sensor. The sensor converts the light into digital form. It is then stored as a file that can be transferred to a computer for later processing. The first portable digital camera was made by Eastman Kodak in 1975. It weighed eight pounds (3.6 kg) and shot only in black-and-white. Digital cameras as we know them today first became popular in the 1990s and early 2000s.

The first portable digital camera was made by Steven Sasson for Eastman Kodak in 1975.

Before digital photography, images were captured on film. Most astrophotographers today have long given up film because of the big advantages of digital. One of the best parts is seeing your photos right away so you can change settings if needed. Another advantage is the large number of shots you can take.

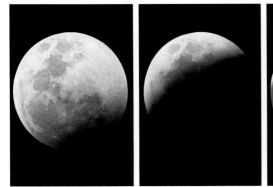  

Modern digital cameras allow photographers to take a large number of shots. This series shows the Moon during a lunar eclipse.

With a DSLR (Digital Single Lens Reflex) camera, you can look through the viewfinder or use the camera's screen display to see exactly what you're shooting.

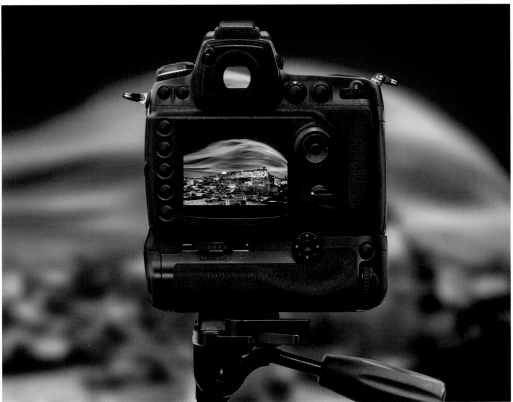

Most amateur astrophotographers today use DSLR (Digital Single Lens Reflex) cameras. With a DSLR, you actually peer through the camera lens so you can see exactly what you're shooting. Angle of view and sharpness are determined by the lens. DSLR lenses are "interchangeable," which means you can change one lens for another depending on your creative needs.

Once light travels inside the DSLR, it is diverted by a mirror upwards into a glass prism. The prism redirects the light into the viewfinder. When you press the shutter release button, the "reflex" mirror flips up and the shutter behind it opens. Light strikes the image sensor. After the exposure, the shutter closes, and the mirror flips back down.

With astrophotography, it is usually difficult to look through the viewfinder. The scene is dark, and it is hard to hunch over with the camera pointed upward toward the sky. Most DSLRs have an LCD screen on the back that makes composing shots and checking exposure much easier. LCD screens use up a lot of power, however, so be sure to bring extra batteries.

The image sensor inside the camera has millions of light-capturing pixels that record an image. The greater the number of pixels, the higher the resolution of the picture. Modern DSLR sensors usually come equipped with at least 16 to 24 megapixels. Some have 40 megapixels or more.

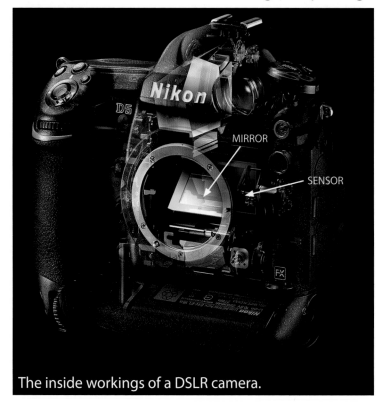

The inside workings of a DSLR camera.

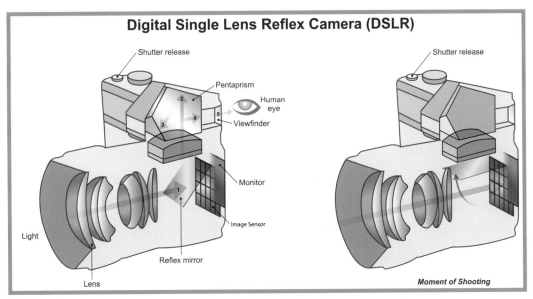

Digital Single Lens Reflex Camera (DSLR)

Shutter release
Pentaprism
Human eye
Viewfinder
Monitor
Image Sensor
Light
Reflex mirror
Lens

Shutter release
Moment of Shooting

This diagram shows how a DSLR camera creates a photograph.

8 TIPS FOR CARING FOR YOUR CAMERA

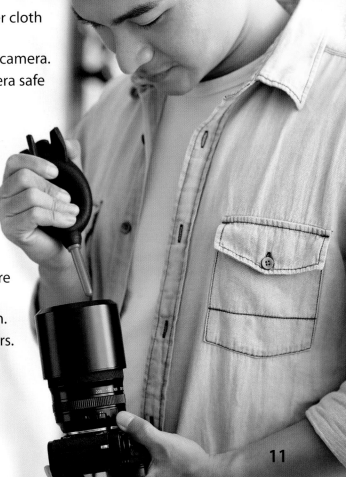

1. Use an air blower and microfiber cloth to clean your camera regularly.
2. Use a strap when carrying your camera.
3. When not in use, keep the camera safe in a bag or case.
4. Use a flashlight or headlamp when walking to set up your camera. You don't want to have an accident, especially in the wilderness. When setting up, switch to red filtered light to preserve your night vision.
5. Make sure you always have spare batteries.
6. Keep your camera out of the rain.
7. Keep your camera out of hot cars.
8. Never leave your camera unattended.

The Canon 6D MkII full-frame DSLR, Nikon D750 full-frame DSLR, and Sony a7 III full-frame mirrorless camera are all excellent for astrophotography.

Nearly any DSLR that you own will work for astrophotography. However, certain camera features will vastly improve your images. Instead of buying a camera with the most megapixels, look for one that produces the least digital noise. Noise is the unwanted signal that the image sensor records. It looks like color banding and tiny specks randomly strewn throughout the picture, like grains of sand. (On film, a similar effect is called "grain.")

Digital noise gets worse with the long exposures and high ISO settings used in astrophotography. You can lessen noise by using full-frame cameras instead of APS (Advanced Photo System) cropped-frame cameras. The sensors in full-frame cameras measure 36x24mm, the same size as a frame of 35mm film. Less-expensive APS cropped-frame cameras use sensors that measure about 23x15mm.

The sensors in cropped-frame cameras use smaller pixels, which produce more digital noise. The sensors in cell phones and GoPro cameras are too small for astrophotography.

The sensors in cropped-frame cameras use smaller pixels, which produce more digital noise. Image-editing software such as Photoshop can reduce the effects of digital noise. However, as your skills grow, you will definitely want to step up to a full-frame camera.

Cell phones and GoPro cameras are not good for astrophotography. Their sensors are too small, and their controls are too difficult to use manually. Mirrorless cameras eliminate the glass prism of DSLRs. They are very light, and some have excellent sensors for astrophotography.

The digital noise is easy to see in this night sky photo.

LENSES

For great astrophotography, you absolutely need a high-quality lens. Fast lenses are preferred, with apertures that open up to around f/2.8 or wider. The more light you let into the camera during exposures, the faster your shutter speed can be (assuming you use the same ISO), which equals less digital noise. Slower lenses, like the kind sold with many camera bodies, can work for moonscapes and twilight shots, but not as well for Milky Way nightscapes.

A lens's field of view is measured in millimeters. A "normal" field of view captured by a full-frame image sensor is about 50mm. That is about the same as what you perceive with your eyes. Common wide-angle lenses are about 24mm to 35mm. Super-wide lenses start at about 10mm. Below that are fisheye lenses, which are used for special effects because of their distortion.

Super-wide lenses are useful for capturing panoramas of the full Milky Way. The focal length on this shot was 14mm.

This wide-angle view of the Milky Way and a moonlit arch was shot with a 20mm focal length lens.

Telephoto lenses start at around 85mm to 105mm. The most common telephoto zoom lenses are about 80-200mm. If you shoot the Moon as it sets or rises, you'll probably want a telephoto lens, about 200mm or more.

For taking nightscapes of the sky and land together, use a wide-angle lens. Popular focal lengths range from about 10mm to 24mm. Whatever lens you use, be sure to *turn off* image stabilization (also called vibration reduction) if your camera or lens has it available. It ruins images taken with tripod-mounted cameras.

FOCUSING

The infinity mark (∞) on your lens doesn't necessarily mean distant stars will be in focus. Sometimes, the sharpest focus point is just a little less than infinity. Before darkness sets in, use autofocus on the horizon. Switch to manual focus and use tape on the focus ring of your lens to keep it in place. Another method is to take a test exposure of the stars and check the LCD screen on the camera's back. Zoom in and check to make sure the brightest stars are in sharp focus.

OTHER EQUIPMENT

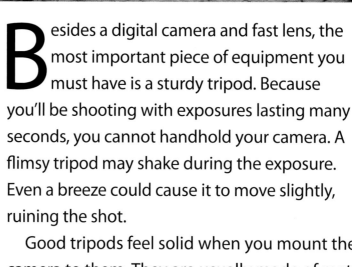

Tripod

Besides a digital camera and fast lens, the most important piece of equipment you must have is a sturdy tripod. Because you'll be shooting with exposures lasting many seconds, you cannot handhold your camera. A flimsy tripod may shake during the exposure. Even a breeze could cause it to move slightly, ruining the shot.

Good tripods feel solid when you mount the camera to them. They are usually made of metal or carbon fiber. The tripod's head (the part where you attach the camera) should be able to point straight up. For extra stability, weigh the tripod down by hanging a bag of rocks or sand to the center column (some center columns have a convenient hook on the end).

Lithium Ion Battery Pack

Remote Shutter Release

Memory Card

Headlamp

A remote shutter release is a must-have accessory. Touching the camera shakes it slightly, causing blur. A remote shutter release consists of a cable that plugs into the camera. A trigger at the end of the cable signals the camera shutter to open. Some cameras have wireless shutter releases available.

Always bring extra batteries. Long exposure times and heavy use of the camera's LCD screen quickly drain batteries.

Remember to bring one or two spare high-capacity memory cards. Also don't forget a flashlight or headlamp with a red and white filter to help preserve your night vision.

CAMERA SETTINGS & EXPOSURE

A mode dial set to "M."

Modern DSLRs are marvels of technology. During daylight shooting, their onboard computers can calculate the proper exposure for the most demanding situations.

Forget all that. For astrophotography, you'll be shooting in manual. But don't worry, it's not that difficult. Turn your mode dial to "M," which stands for manual. To set shutter speed and aperture, spin the scroll wheels on top of your camera. Check your camera's instruction manual for details. Get familiar with the controls, because you'll be adjusting them in the dark.

Set your camera to shoot in RAW format instead of JPEG. RAW collects all the data captured by the image sensor and saves it in a file.

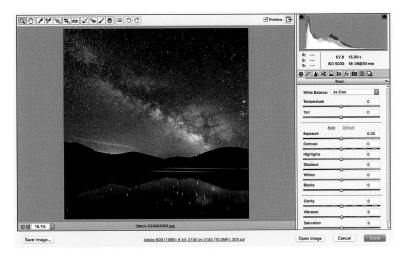

A screen shot of Adobe's Camera RAW photo editor.

You process it later with image editing software. If you shoot in JPEG format, the camera processes the image and throws away much of the data. In order to save the delicate details of far-away stars and nebulas, you need all of the data your camera collects. Plus, if your photo is under or overexposed, or the color balance is off, it is very easy to fix in RAW.

There are many online tutorials and books that can teach you how to process RAW images. It is a skill that is well worth the effort in order to get the most out of your astrophotography images.

RAW + JPEG

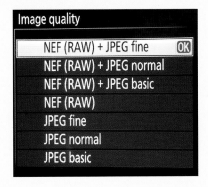

If you want to share your images online right away, even before processing them, you can always set your camera to record RAW plus JPEG at the same time. This setting may be convenient, but remember that it will take up more space on your memory card, since the camera is writing two files at once.

A camera lens's aperture.

Three things determine your exposure for night photography: shutter speed, aperture, and ISO. Adjusting each one brings advantages and trade-offs.

Aperture is the size of your lens opening. The wider the opening, the more light is let in to strike the image sensor. Aperture settings are measured in f-stops. The smaller the number, the bigger the lens opening (the opposite of what someone might expect). A fast lens (one that has a very large aperture) starts at about f/2.8. Some open even wider, and can be very expensive.

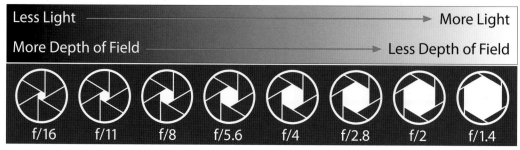

Less Light	→	More Light
More Depth of Field	→	Less Depth of Field

| f/16 | f/11 | f/8 | f/5.6 | f/4 | f/2.8 | f/2 | f/1.4 |

Typical lens f-stop settings.

Aperture also controls depth of field. This is the range of distance (depth), from front to back, that is in sharp focus in your image. The wider the lens opening, the shallower the depth of field. However, since almost all astrophotography is of distant landscapes and stars, controlling depth of field is less important. You can set your lens to its widest aperture to let in the most light during the exposure and not worry about the shallow depth of field.

With some lenses, aberrations become more apparent at the widest aperture settings. Along the edges of the picture, stars might appear blurry and distorted (stretched out). Fringes of green or purple colors can also seem to seep out of the stars (chromatic aberration). Much lens aberration can be corrected in Photoshop, Lightroom, or other photo editing software.

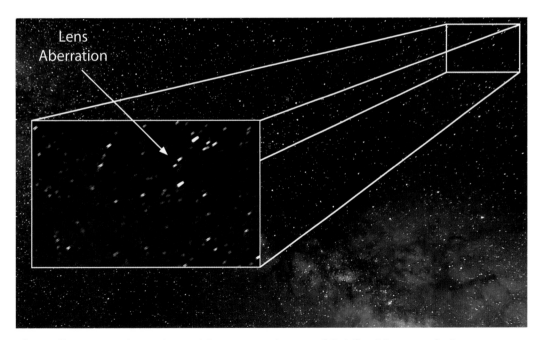

The Milky Way galaxy shot with a 24mm lens at f/2.8 for 20 seconds. Lens aberrations, such as the stretched out stars shown in the enlargement, often appear on the edge of the frame, when a lens is opened to its widest aperture.

Shutter speed is the length of time the camera's shutter opens to let light strike the image sensor. It is measured in seconds (usually a fraction of a second). In astrophotography, the longer the shutter speed the better, up until the point where you start to get star trails. This blurring effect happens because the Earth is rotating as the shutter is open, and the stationary stars "streak" across the image sensor. It is most noticeable on long exposures, usually 20 seconds or more, but depends on your lens's focal length.

Wider focal length lenses can stay open longer without causing too much of a star trail effect. A general rule for finding the longest shutter speed without noticeable star trails is to take 500 divided by the focal length of your lens. For example, 500/24 (for a 24mm lens) equals a shutter speed of about 21 seconds. Anything longer than this, and star trails will start to become too noticeable.

Astrophotographers shoot the night sky and review the images on a laptop screen.

A magnified section of the above night sky photo shows noticeable blurry star trails. It was shot with a 35mm lens at f/1.4 for 30 seconds.

ISO is the last piece of the exposure puzzle. It is the image sensor's sensitivity to light. If you double the ISO number, the sensor only needs half as much light to make the same exposure. That lets you shoot with smaller apertures and shorter shutter speeds. The trade-off is that more digital noise is apparent in photos made with high ISO numbers. Fortunately, much of the noise can be minimized with image editing software such as Photoshop or Lightroom.

COMPOSITION

Much of how you compose your astrophotography images depends on the kind of event you're trying to capture. For nightscapes, which include both the land below and the starry sky above, basic rules of composition apply. Use the rule of thirds for a pleasing, balanced effect.

Good Earth-bound subjects to include in your foreground include mountains, trees, barns, churches, lakes, and many other objects. If you are shooting in North America, you will probably be standing to the north or east of the subject, shooting astronomical objects to the south and west. Scout your locations during the daytime to figure out the best place to set up your tripod. Free computer software such as Stellarium can help you find out beforehand exactly where the Moon and Milky Way will be during your photo shoot.

Much of your success will depend on timing. For the darkest skies, shoot during the new Moon. The landscape will be in silhouette. For landscape detail, shoot during a crescent Moon. The Milky Way is visible in North America from about June through September. Weather, of course, will also affect your images. Try to arrange your photo expeditions when the forecasts call for clear, dry evenings.

THE RULE OF THIRDS

The "rule of thirds" is a way of dividing the viewfinder into sections and arranging your subject within the lines. Divide your viewfinder into three horizontal parts, and three vertical parts. Put your subject roughly near one of the intersecting lines. Since the sky is your main subject, most nightscapes are composed so it occupies the top two-thirds of the image. Instead of a "rule," think of it as a helpful guideline. Oftentimes, putting your subject off-center makes the composition more pleasing and interesting.

TWILIGHT

During twilight, in the minutes after sunset, the sky is awash with deep, delicate colors. Look for tints of red, orange, blue, and even purple. Some of the best colors occur when you think it's too dark. Keep shooting with longer shutter speeds. Later in the digital darkroom, you'll be able to bring out spectacular color images.

Photo was shot with a 300mm lens, exposed at f/8 for .4 second.

TWILIGHT CAMERA SETTINGS

Aperture
For twilight, you can get by with slower lenses that have maximum apertures of f/2.8 to f/5.6.

ISO
Slower ISO speeds, down to 100 or 200, will help minimize the apparent digital noise that often shows up in twilight skies.

Shutter Speed
Experiment. You'll be using a tripod, so long shutter speeds are fine. You'll usually be shooting at under 30 seconds.

MOONRISE AND MOONSET

Together with the twilight sky, a rising or setting Moon is one of the easiest astronomical scenes to shoot. Beautiful by itself or accompanying a landscape or cityscape scene, the Moon is a dramatic object that has many moods. To fill the frame as much as possible with the Moon, you'll need a long telephoto lens. The Moon is much smaller in reality than it appears to our eyes. For landscapes, use a moderate telephoto focal length, such as 200mm. To plan where the Moon will rise and set, you can use astronomy software such as Starry Night, Sky Safari, PhotoPills, Sun Surveyor, and others.

Photo was shot with a 200mm lens, exposed at f/14 for 10 seconds.

Photo was shot with a 800mm lens, exposed at f/7.1 for 1/125 second.

MOONRISE AND MOONSET CAMERA SETTINGS

Aperture
The Moon is a sunlit object, so you'll need to stop down your lens aperture. Start with f/4 or f/5.6.

ISO
There is plenty of twilight at moonrise and moonset, so set your ISO to 100 or 200 to minimize digital noise.

Shutter Speed
With your camera on a tripod for sharp results, experiment with shutter speeds. Most will be around one second or less.

THE MILKY WAY

On dark, moonless nights far from glowing cities, the Milky Way becomes visible in the inky sky. Shaped like a spiral disk that bulges in the middle, the Milky Way is our home galaxy. It contains about 100 billion stars. Our solar system is on the galaxy's edge. When we spy the glowing lights at night, we are looking inward toward the galaxy's center. The Milky Way's central core is visible in North America from about June through September.

Photo was shot with a 24mm lens, exposed at f/2.8 for 18 seconds.

MILKY WAY CAMERA SETTINGS

Lens and Aperture
Use a wide-angle lens, about 14 to 24mm. It is important that it have a very wide aperture. A fast lens shot at f/2.8, f/2, or wider is ideal.

ISO
Start with an ISO of 1600. You may need to increase it to 3200 or even 6400.

Shutter Speed
The goal is to have the longest shutter speed possible without obvious star trails. Start with 15 seconds, then try 20 and 30 seconds. You may have to go all the way up to 60 seconds, but expect blurry star trails.

Photo was shot with a 17mm lens, exposed at f/4 for 20 seconds.

Photo was shot with an 18mm lens, exposed at f/2.8 for 25 seconds.

METEOR SHOWERS

Meteors, also called shooting stars, are rocks from space (meteoroids) that burn up in Earth's atmosphere. They are more common during annual meteor showers. The Perseid meteor shower occurs each August, with about 90 lights streaking across the sky every hour. Capturing meteors takes patience and luck.

METEOR CAMERA SETTINGS

Lens and Aperture
Use a wide-angle lens at an aperture of f/2.8 or wider.

ISO
Meteors are best captured during dark, moonless nights. Set your ISO to 800 or higher.

Shutter Speed
Start off with 20 seconds, then take a series of images to maximize your chance of catching a meteor as it streaks by. If you don't mind star trails, you can increase your shutter speed up to about a minute.

AURORAS

The aurora borealis, or the Northern Lights, are delicate curtains of light that ripple across the sky. Normally seen in far northern latitudes, they are caused by charged particles from the Sun (the solar wind) striking Earth's atmosphere. (In the southern hemisphere, they are called the aurora australis.)

Photo was shot with a 20mm lens, exposed at f/2.8 for 15 seconds.

AURORA CAMERA SETTINGS

Lens and Aperture
Very wide-angle lenses give great results, capturing the aurora as it stretches across the sky. Use an aperture of f/2.8 or wider.

ISO
Your ISO setting ranges from 400 to 3200.

Shutter Speed
From about 15 to 20 seconds. If the aurora seems dim, shoot longer. Hidden colors and detail can be brought out by the camera.

STAR TRAILS

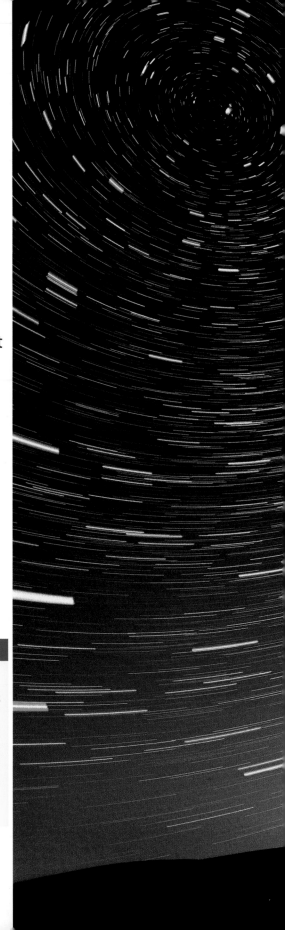

Although normally avoided, sometimes star trails can create a beautiful nightscape effect. The rings of light remind us of the vastness of our universe, and the wonders of the night sky. Successful star trail astrophotography is difficult to master. If you're a beginner, get help, or wait until you have more experience shooting easier subjects such as twilight or the Milky Way. The basic technique is to take a series of long exposures over a period of hours. The photos are then stacked together, usually with computer software such as StarStaX, which creates long star trails.

STAR TRAILS CAMERA SETTINGS		
Aperture	**ISO**	**Shutter Speed**
Shoot wide open at f/2.8 or wider, or try one stop higher to reduce lens aberrations.	Between 800 and 1600.	For many shorter exposures (100 or more), try a shutter speed of 30 seconds. To shoot a single frame, or several long shots stacked together, leave the shutter open for up to 1 hour.

Photo is a single 24-minute exposure.

LIGHT PAINTING

Light painting is a technique that combines traditional nightscape photography with slow-shutter light sculpting. While the shutter is open, you take a bright LED flashlight and wave the beam across the foreground scene, "painting" it with light. The result can be very dramatic, which has made this technique popular in recent years. It takes trial and error to know just how much light to use to create a nicely exposed foreground. Paint from the sides to avoid giving the scene that flat "direct flash" look. Also, be aware that you are creating light pollution. Be courteous if other photographers are present.

LIGHT PAINTING CAMERA SETTINGS

Aperture	ISO	Shutter Speed
For dark, moonless nights, open your lens to its maximum aperture of f/2.8 or wider.	800 to 6400, depending on the scene you're photographing.	Between 20 and 30 seconds to give you plenty of time for light painting. Anything longer will result in noticeable star trails.

Photo was shot with a 22mm lens,
exposed at f/2.8 for 25 seconds.

A composite of the August 21, 2017, total solar eclipse.

SOLAR ECLIPSES

A solar eclipse happens when the Moon moves precisely in front of the Sun, blocking most of its light. They are rare events for any particular spot on Earth, but happen often enough that most people should be able to experience a solar eclipse at least once in their life. To photograph it, you'll need a DSLR, a good lens, and a sturdy tripod. Many people try to fill the frame with the eclipse by using a telephoto lens, but interesting landscapes and time-lapse images can also be taken with wide-angle lenses. When photographing solar eclipses, special filters are required to protect your camera and especially your eyes. Get a responsible adult to help you with these kinds of photographs.

DEEP SKY

Equatorial Mount

Deep-sky astrophotography focuses on objects beyond our solar system, including star clusters, galaxies, and nebulae. Equipment can be highly specialized, with cameras, lenses, telescopes, and other gear costing thousands of dollars. However, good images can be taken with normal DSLRs. One vital piece of equipment is a motorized equatorial tracking mount. With the camera mounted on top, it rotates and automatically compensates for the Earth's rotation. This eliminates star trails caused by long exposures. Pictures can be taken through telescopes or long telephoto lenses. Deep-sky astrophotography is a rewarding hobby that can last a lifetime.

The Horsehead Nebula.

THE DIGITAL DARKROOM

Pictures straight out of the camera are often disappointing. What many beginners don't realize is that most nightscape photos don't really pop until they've been processed in the digital darkroom. Modern software can bring out the delicate structures and colors that are hiding inside the RAW files produced by your camera. Color balance, sharpening, saturation, white balance, noise reduction, and cropping are the most important enhancements. These are all easy to perform with software such as Photoshop, Lightroom, or GIMP.

Image editing software can be hard to learn, but it is a fun way to improve your photos. Use the software's help menus, or search for online video instructions. Everyone was a beginner once, and many generous photographers are happy to share their skills.

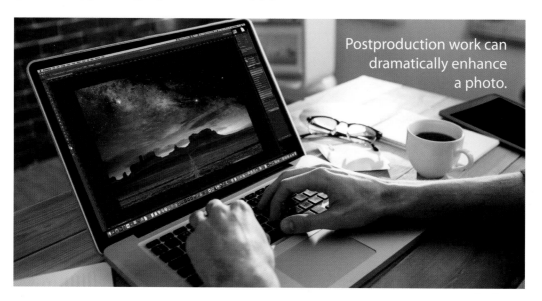

Postproduction work can dramatically enhance a photo.

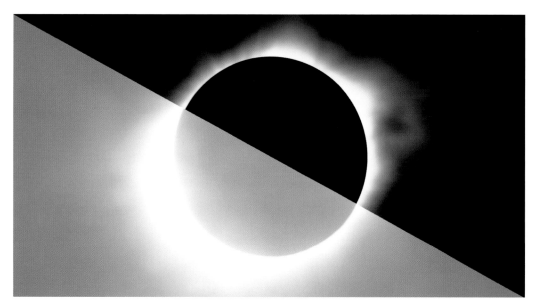

Almost every nightscape photo can be made better with image processing software such as Photoshop or Lightroom. The photo above shows a full solar eclipse before and after image processing to improve contrast and color. The photo below shows the Cat's Paw Nebula before and after digital processing. Color balance, contrast, saturation, and noise reduction were all improved, bringing out the fine details and vibrant colors of this star-forming gas cloud.

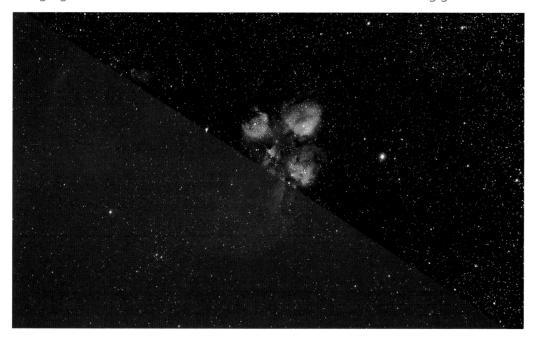

BACKING UP YOUR PHOTOS

Make copies of your digital images. Keep them safe on at least two storage devices. All hard drives will fail eventually. Without a backup, your photos will vanish, representing many months, perhaps years, of hard work.

In most professional studios, photos are backed up on several different devices. In addition to the hard drive on your main computer, use backup software every day to automatically copy all your photos onto a portable hard drive. These small devices get cheaper every year, with bigger capacities. Every few days or weeks, swap out the external drive with one that you might keep in a safe deposit box at your bank. This strategy is called having an off-site backup. If disaster strikes, such as your house burning down or washing away in a flood, your work will remain safe.

Portable hard drives hold a lot of photos and can be kept in different locations as off-site backups.

PORTABLE
HARD DRIVE

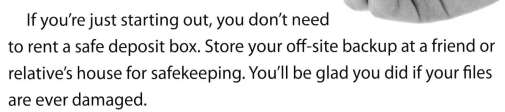

A USB flash drive is an easy and portable way to back up your photographs. It is a good device to use when traveling.

If you're just starting out, you don't need to rent a safe deposit box. Store your off-site backup at a friend or relative's house for safekeeping. You'll be glad you did if your files are ever damaged.

Some photographers store off-site backups in the Cloud. That means using the Internet to automatically store digital copies on large computer servers run by companies such as Dropbox, Apple, or Google. Cloud storage can be impractical because digital photo collections often grow to many gigabytes in size and could take days to upload. However, technology changes rapidly, and Cloud storage becomes more appealing with each passing year.

For extra protection, you can also keep your best files backed up on USB flash drives. After copying, toss them in a desk drawer. It's probably not totally necessary, but it'll give you peace of mind.

COPYRIGHT

Who owns your photos? You do, of course. The moment you press the shutter release button, you own the copyright to that image. To get even more protection, you can register your photos for a fee with the U.S. Copyright Office in Washington, DC, at copyright.gov. Registered or not, nobody has the right to use your images without your permission.

ASTROPHOTOGRAPHY QUICK START

The following settings are good starting points for most DSLR cameras. The actual settings that work best for you will depend on your location, the weather, and your creative tastes.

IF YOU ARE SHOOTING...

	Twilight	Moon	Milky Way
Shutter Speed	1/125 to 30 sec	1/400 to 1 sec	15 to 30 sec
ISO	100 to 200	100 to 200	1600 to 6400
Aperture	f/2.8 to f/5.6	f/4 to f/5.6	f/2.8 or wider

OTHER SETTINGS

Camera
Shoot in RAW format, or RAW + JPEG. Auto exposure off. Aperture and shutter speed set to manual.

Lens
Image stabilization (vibration reduction) off. Autofocus off.

In-Camera Noise Reduction
Turn off noise reduction if making star trails. (It's better to reduce noise in Photoshop or Lightroom.) Otherwise, may leave on.

White Balance
Depends on location. With dark skies, set to 3,500 to 4,500 Kelvin. Otherwise, leave on auto. Images shot in RAW format are easily changed in Photoshop or Lightroom.

GLOSSARY

APERTURE
The opening in the lens that lets light pass through to the image sensor. The aperture is usually adjustable, and measured in f-stops.

DIGITAL NOISE
Noise is a collection of digital artifacts, which look like clumps of grains of sand that aren't really part of the scene. It occurs most often in low-light situations where the camera sensor is set with a high ISO number.

DIGITAL SINGLE LENS REFLEX (DSLR)
A digital single lens reflex camera is a kind of camera that features interchangeable lenses and sophisticated electronics. It captures images on a digital image sensor instead of film.

F-STOP
A number that is used to tell the size of a lens's opening, or aperture. Small numbers, such as f/2.8, represent a large aperture. Small apertures, which let in less light, include f/16 and f/22.

ISO NUMBER
A number that describes a camera sensor's sensitivity to light. Cameras that can shoot with high ISO numbers can capture images in very dim lighting conditions. The name ISO is the abbreviation for the International Organization for Standardization, a Swiss company. ISO is not an acronym for the company name. It is the root of the Greek word *isos*, which means "equal." It is pronounced "EYE-so."

KELVIN SCALE
The Kelvin scale is a way of measuring temperature, like Celsius or Fahrenheit. In photography, it is used to define color temperature.

Daylight has a color temperature of 5,600 K. Temperatures below this, such as a 3,200 K tungsten light bulb, appear reddish. Higher Kelvin temperatures appear blueish. Cameras can auto correct color temperature (white balance) so that objects appear neutral white.

LIGHT POLLUTION

Artificial light during the night, caused by automobile lights, street lamps, the burning of natural gas in oil fields, and other sources. Besides affecting human physical and mental health, too much light pollution makes it very difficult to photograph the night sky.

RAW

The RAW image format for cameras contains almost all the data captured by the image sensor. The photo is unprocessed by the camera, which preserves data. Astrophotography images saved in RAW format are later processed with software such as Photoshop and Lightroom. Because all the data is saved, delicate hues and textures can be enhanced and made more visible.

SHARPENING

Although the human eye can detect lines of contrast in a scene with amazing sharpness, camera sensors are limited by the number of pixels they contain. This causes pictures to appear a little out of focus. Cameras and image editing software can "sharpen" images to make them appear almost as sharp as they seem to the eye.

ONLINE RESOURCES

Booklinks
NONFICTION NETWORK
FREE! ONLINE NONFICTION RESOURCES

To learn more about astrophotography, visit abdobooklinks.com. These links are routinely monitored and updated to provide the most current information available.

INDEX